Bc

IN RECITAL®
with Classical Themes
Volume One

ABOUT THE SERIES • A NOTE TO THE TEACHER

In Recital® with Classical Themes is devoted to timeless classical music. The fine arrangers of this series were commissioned to create engaging solo and duet arrangements of classical themes, according to strict pedagogical guidelines. The result is a series that is artistically strong, carefully leveled, and pedagogically sound. We know that to motivate, the teacher must challenge the student with attainable goals. This series makes that possible while also providing a perfect way for students to discover and enjoy classical music themes. You will find favorite themes from symphonies, operas, chamber music, choral music, as well as from advanced piano concertos and piano duets. This series complements other FJH publications and can be used alongside any method. Students will find even more joy in these classical themes when they read about the pieces (a brief history is provided at the beginning and end of each book).

 Use the enclosed CD as a teaching and motivational tool. Have your students listen to the recording and discuss interpretation with you! Also encourage your students to listen to the works in their original format.

Production: Frank J. Hackinson
Production Coordinators: Joyce Loke and Philip Groeber
Art Direction: Terpstra Design, San Francisco, in collaboration with Helen Marlais
Cover and Inside Illustrations: Keith Criss
Engraving: Tempo Music Press, Inc.
Printer: Tempo Music Press, Inc.

ISBN 1-56939-650-7

ORGANIZATION OF THE SERIES
IN RECITAL® WITH CLASSICAL THEMES

The series is carefully leveled into the following six categories: Early Elementary, Elementary, Late Elementary, Early Intermediate, Intermediate, and Late Intermediate. Each of the works has been selected for its artistic as well as its pedagogical merit.

Book One — Early Elementary, reinforces the following concepts:

- Basic notes such as quarter, half, dotted half, and whole notes are used.

- $\frac{3}{4}$ and $\frac{4}{4}$ time signatures.

- Students experience movement up and down the keyboard, with *8va* signs.

- Students play with both a detached and smooth touch.

- Most of the pieces call for limited use of hands-together playing.

- Pieces reinforce basic musical terminology and symbols such as *forte*, *piano*, *mezzo forte*, *mezzo piano*, repeat signs, *loco*, *descrescendo*, tied notes, and *fermata*.

- Pieces use middle C and G position as well as other basic hand positions.

- Keys — C major, G major, F major, and A minor (written using accidentals instead of key signatures).

Most of the classical themes in this book were arranged as solos. Some of them include teacher accompaniments.

FF1697

TABLE OF CONTENTS

	Recital Category	Composer	Arranger	Page	CD Track
About the Pieces and Composers				4-5	
Eine kleine Nachtmusik (*A Little Night Music*, K. 525, Movement One)	Optional Duet	Wolfgang Amadeus Mozart	Edwin McLean	6-9	1
Berceuse from *Dolly Suite*, *Opus 56, No. 1*	Solo	Gabriel Fauré	Kevin Olson	10-11	2
The Harmonious Blacksmith from *Air with 5 Variations* from *Suite in E major*, *No. 148*	Optional Duet	George Frideric Handel	Mary Leaf	12-13	3
The Great Gate of Kiev from *Pictures at an Exhibition*	Optional Duet	Modest Petrovich Mussorgsky	Kevin Olson	14-15	4
Barcarolle from *The Tales of Hoffmann*	Solo	Jacques Offenbach	Robert Schultz	16-18	5
Merry Widow Waltz from *Die lustige Witwe*	Optional Duet	Franz Lehár	Timothy Brown	19-21	6
Alleluia from *Exsultate, jubilate*, K. 165	Solo	Wolfgang Amadeus Mozart	Timothy Brown	22-23	7
"Surprise" Symphony (*Symphony in G major*, Hob. 94, Movement Two)	Optional Duet	Franz Joseph Haydn	Mary Leaf	24-25	8
Finlandia (*Opus 26*)	Solo	Jean Sibelius	Kevin Costley	26-27	9
Roses from the South *Waltz 2 from Das Spitzentuch der Königin*, *Opus 388*	Optional Duet	Johann Strauss II	Edwin McLean	28-29	10
Theme from *L'Arlésienne Suite*	Unequal Part Duet	Georges Bizet	Emilie Lin	30-33	11
About the Pieces and Composers				34-35	
About the Arrangers				36-38	
Fun with Classical Themes				39	

ABOUT THE PIECES AND COMPOSERS

Eine kleine Nachtmusik, by Wolfgang Amadeus Mozart (1756-1791)

Mozart composed *A Little Night Music* for string quartet. A string quartet is an important chamber music ensemble made up of two violinists, a violist, and a cellist. *A Little Night Music* has five movements, or sections. After each movement the performers rest briefly before they begin the next movement. If you were watching and listening to musicians play this piece, you would only clap at the very end of the piece, not after each movement. Mozart wrote this famous piece while living in Vienna and it was completed on August 10, 1787. During this time he was also writing one of his most famous operas, *Don Giovanni*.

Berceuse, by Gabriel Fauré (1845-1924)

A *berceuse* is a lullaby. Can you hear this when you listen to the CD recording? This lullaby is part of a larger work, called the *Dolly Suite* and was written for the piano. It consists of six pieces: 1) *Berceuse,* 2) *Mi-a-ou,* 3) *Dolly's Garden,* 4) *Kitty Waltz,* 5) *Tenderness,* and 6) *The Spanish Dance.* Gabriel Fauré's many accomplishments influenced the course of French music. As a composer, teacher, pianist, and organist, he is widely regarded as the greatest master of French song. He was gifted, handsome, kind, and well liked. In 1905 he became the director of the Conservatory in Paris, France, and was a famous teacher of composers.

The Harmonious Blacksmith, by George Frideric Handel (1685-1759)

The Harmonious Blacksmith consists of a theme along with a set of variations. George Frideric Handel wrote this famous piece for the harpsichord. In this book, you will play a piano arrangement of the main theme. Handel was born in Halle, Germany and was one of the most important composers of his time. Handel's father did not want his son to be a musician, but he was so motivated and disciplined in the subject that his father finally gave in and let him follow his destiny. Handel lived for a time in Italy, learning how to compose opera, chamber music, and vocal music. Then he moved to England, and earned a lifetime pension from Queen Anne. Handel is especially known for writing oratorios, which are large works for chorus and orchestra. His most famous oratorio the *Messiah,* was composed in 1745.

The Great Gate of Kiev, by Modest Petrovich Mussorgsky (1839-1881)

The Great Gate of Kiev is part of a larger work titled *Pictures at an Exhibition*. There is a story as well as a picture behind each of the ten pieces. *The Great Gate of Kiev* was inspired by a design created for a grand gateway that was never constructed. When you listen to this piece, imagine a magnificent procession passing through a gate. You should play it grandly and majestically. *Pictures at an Exhibition* for advanced pianists was published in late 1886 to early 1887. Mussorgsky had extraordinary abilities as a self-taught composer, having an exceptional gift for learning by absorbing the works of others. He believed in celebrating Russian legends and history through music.

Barcarolle, by Jacques Offenbach (1819-1880)

A *barcarolle* is a "boat song," typically written in triple time. Originally, barcarolles were songs sung by men who would steer gondolas in Venice, Italy. If you go to Venice today, there are still gondolas and men who sing as they row through the many canals of the city. This particular piece is from an operetta called *The Tales of Hoffmann*. It was written by a French composer named Offenbach. He was also a conductor and virtuoso cellist. He wrote over ninety operettas, which are short operas with light and cheerful subject matter. The melodies are happy and tuneful. The operetta became internationally known and led to the twentieth-century musical.

Merry Widow Waltz, by Franz Lehár (1870-1948)

This cheerful theme is from an operetta (a short and light opera) that was premiered (first performed) in Vienna in 1905. It is a story of romance and intrigue that has been popular throughout the world ever since its premiere. Franz Lehár was from Hungary and his first music instructor was his father, a military bandmaster. Like his father, Lehár conducted various army bands before he was appointed conductor of the musical theater in Vienna. Listen for the feel of a waltz while you play this joyful piece.

EINE KLEINE NACHTMUSIK

(A Little Night Music, K. 525, Movement One)

Wolfgang Amadeus Mozart
arr. Edwin McLean

Allegro (♩ = ca. 132)

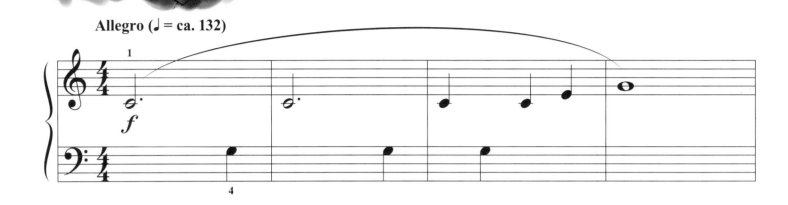

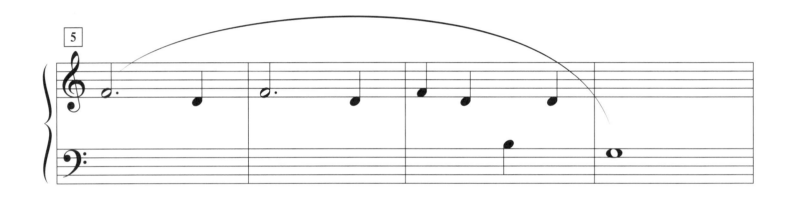

Teacher Accompaniment: (*Student plays one octave higher*)

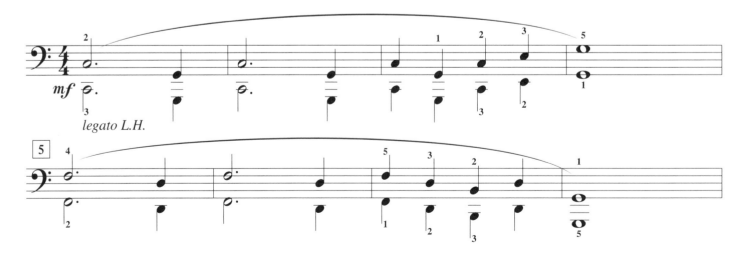

FF1697

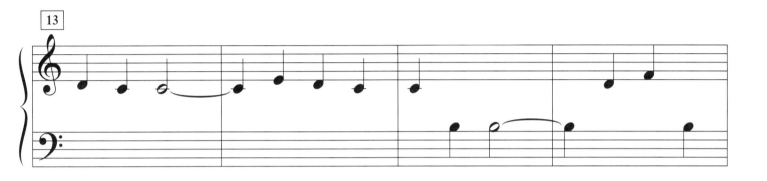

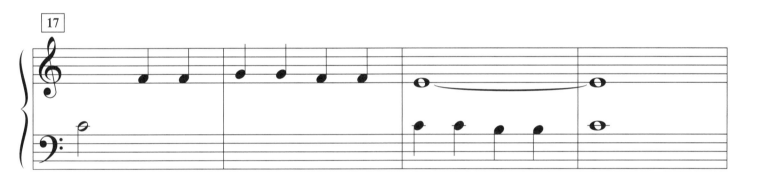

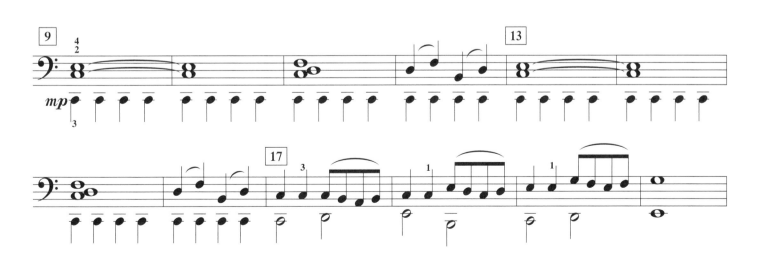

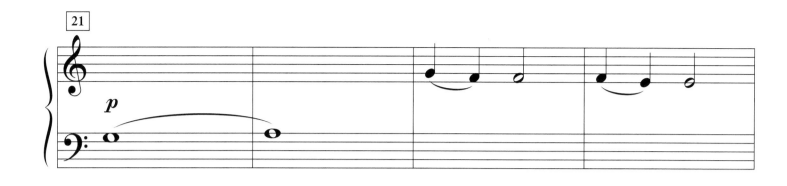

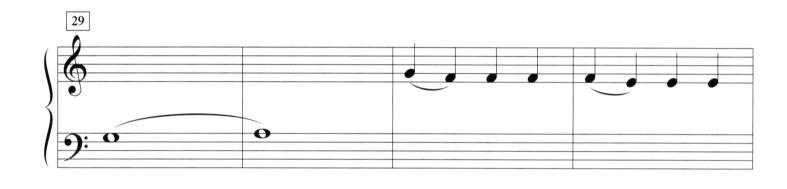

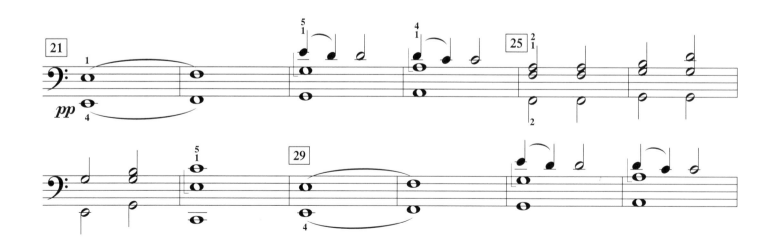

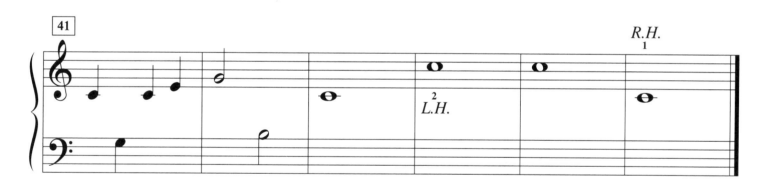

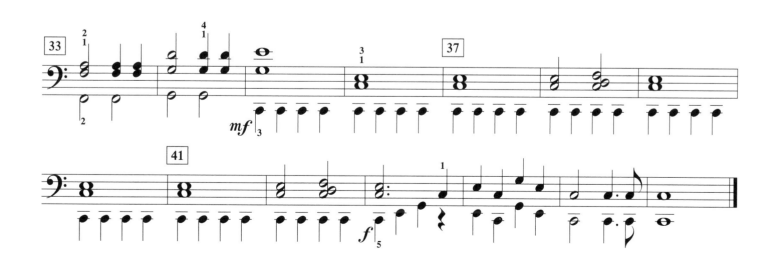

BERCEUSE
from *Dolly Suite, Opus 56, No. 1*

Gabriel Fauré
arr. Kevin Olson

Allegretto moderato (♩ = 138)

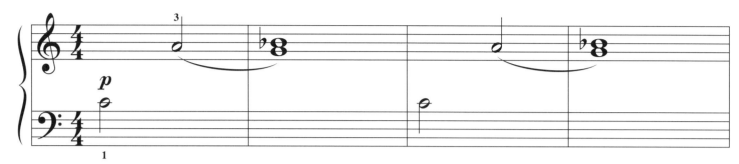

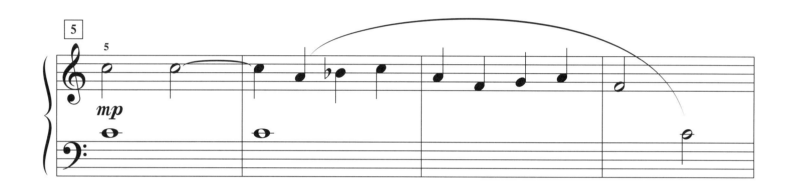

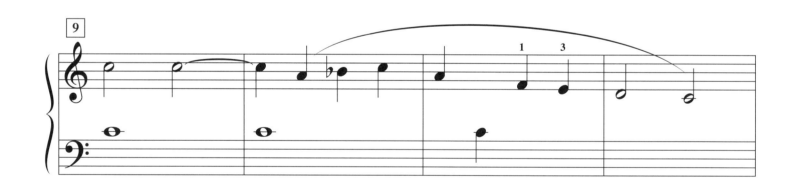

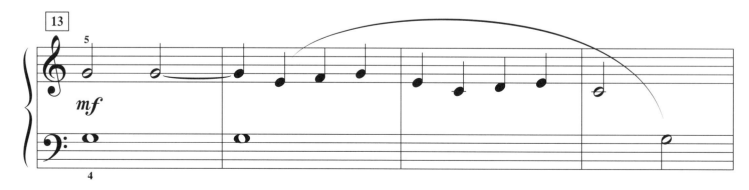

FF1697

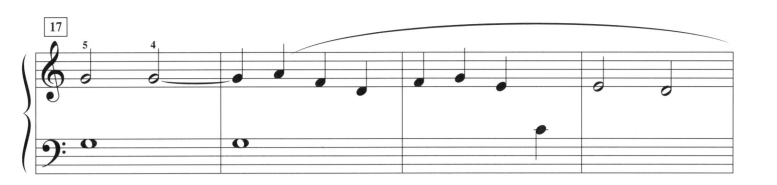

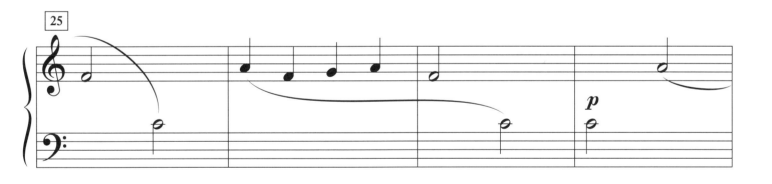

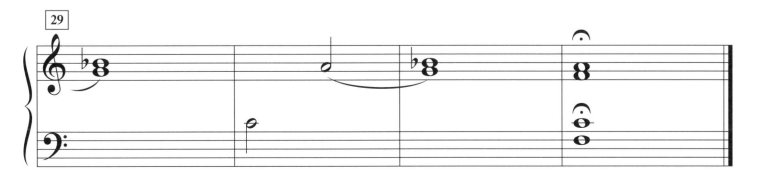

THE HARMONIOUS BLACKSMITH

from *Air with 5 Variations* from *Suite in E major, No. 148*

George Frideric Handel
arr. Mary Leaf

Teacher Accompaniment: (*Student plays one octave higher*)

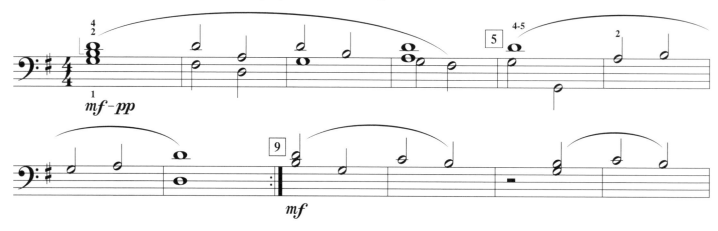

FF1697

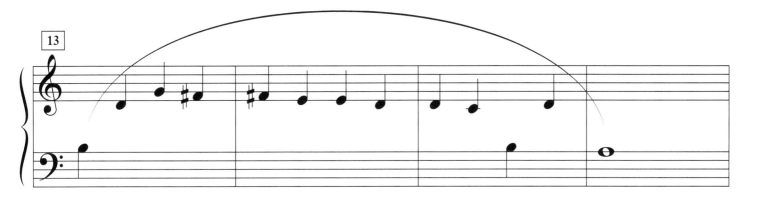

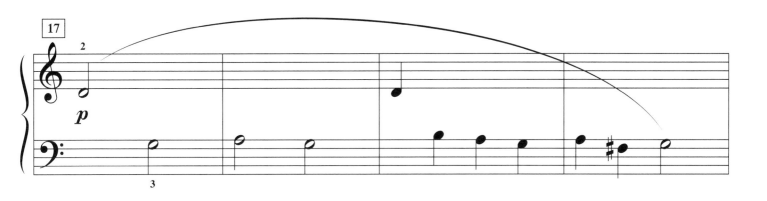

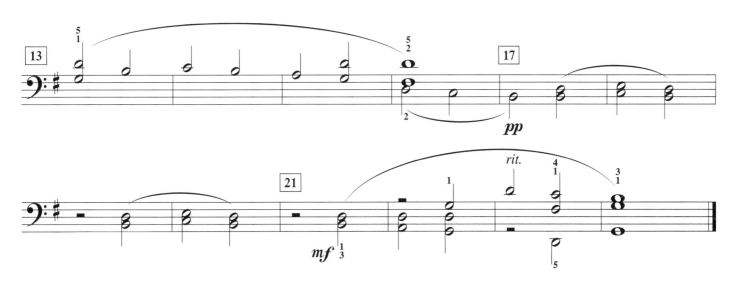

THE GREAT GATE OF KIEV

from *Pictures at an Exhibition*

Modest Petrovich Mussorgsky
arr. Kevin Olson

Maestoso con grandeza (♩ = ca. 120)

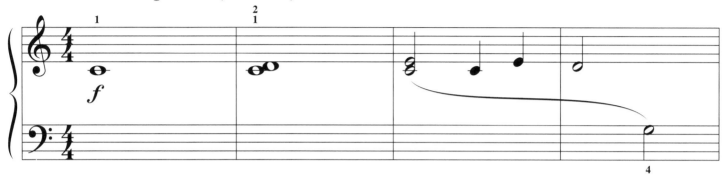

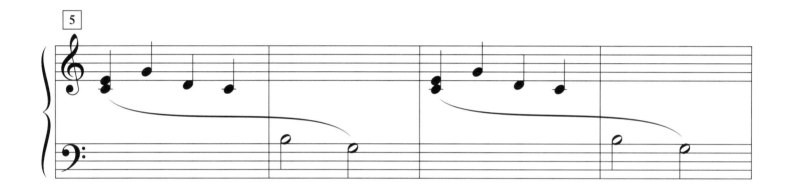

Teacher Accompaniment: (*Student plays one octave higher*)

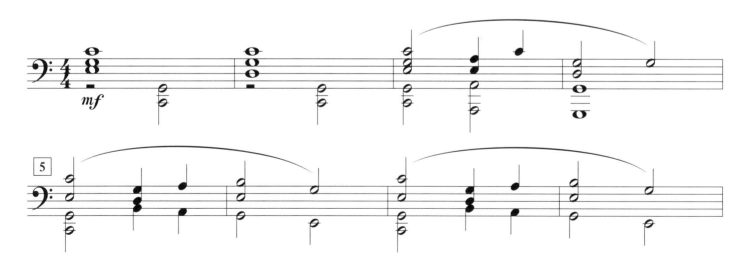

FF1697

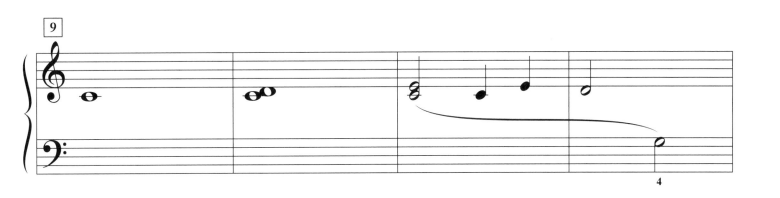

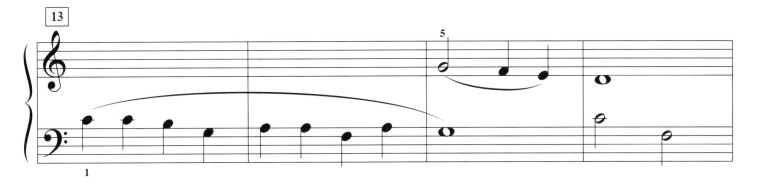

BARCAROLLE
from *The Tales of Hoffmann*

Jacques Offenbach
arr. Robert Schultz

Moderato (♩. = ca. 63)

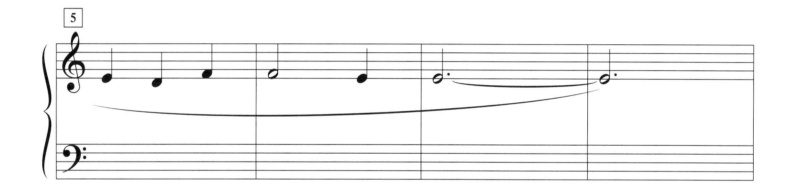

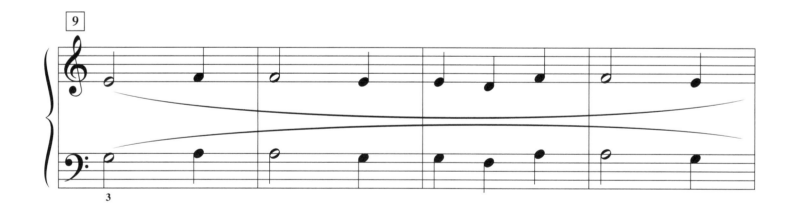

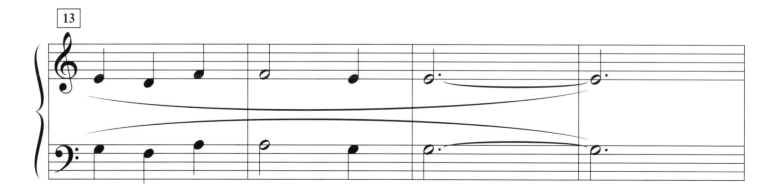

FF1697

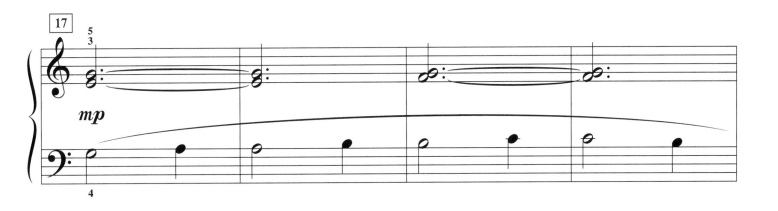

(prepare to move R.H. up)

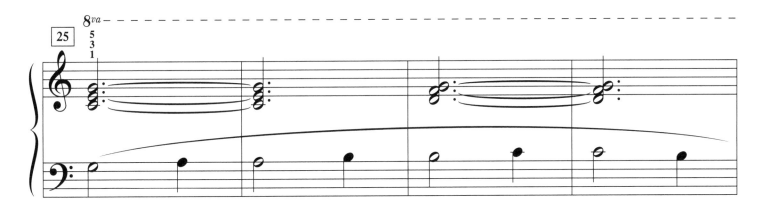

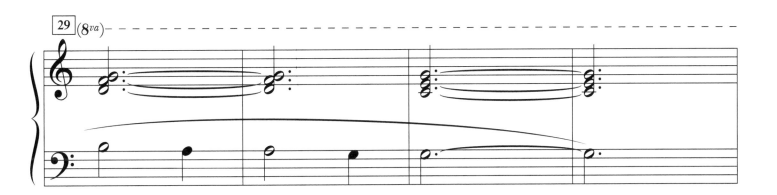

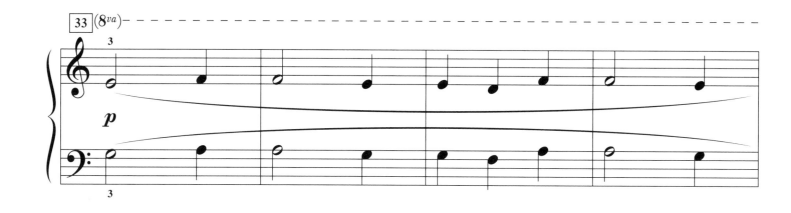

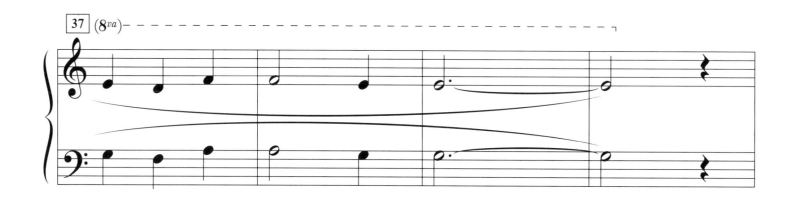

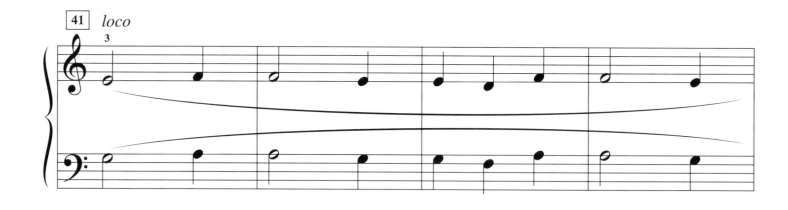

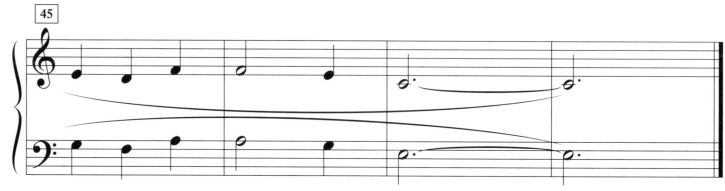

N.B. The Italian term *loco* means to go back to the original octave.

FF1697

MERRY WIDOW WALTZ

from *Die lustige Witwe*

Franz Lehár
arr. Timothy Brown

Happily (♩. = ca. 72)

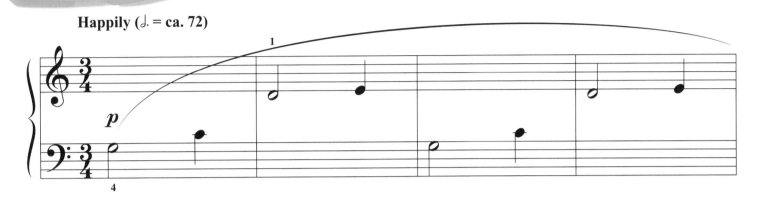

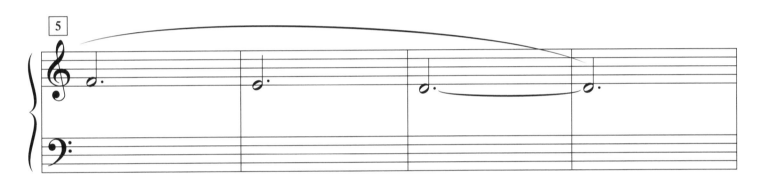

Teacher Accompaniment: *(Student plays one octave higher)*

FF1697

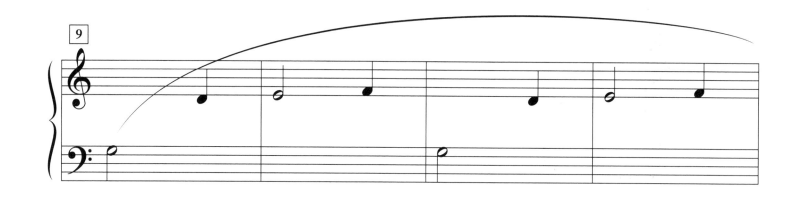

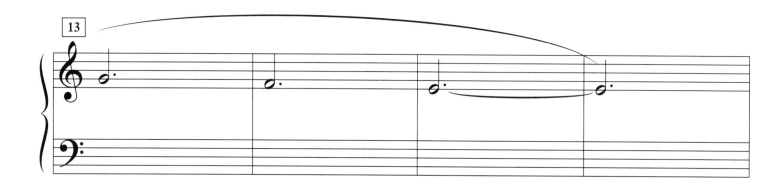

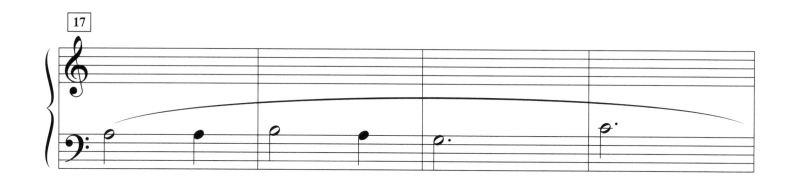

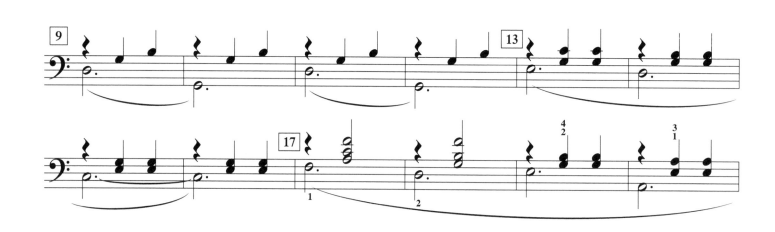

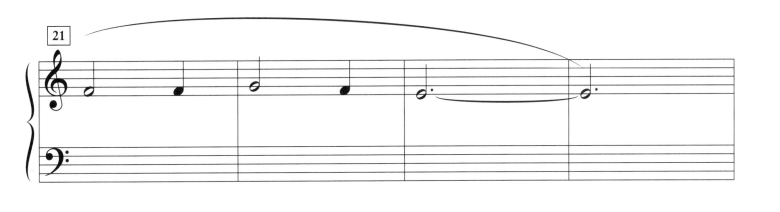

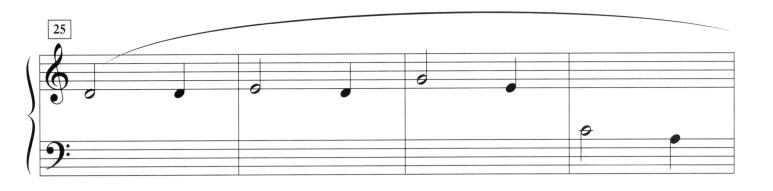

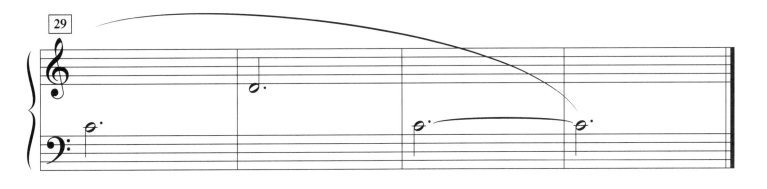

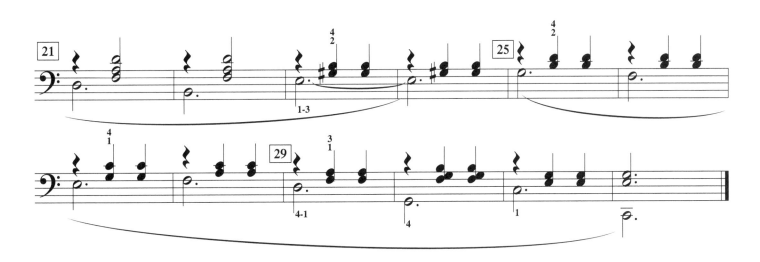

ALLELUIA

from *Exsultate, jubilate*, K. 165

Wolfgang Amadeus Mozart
arr. Timothy Brown

Molto allegro (♩ = ca. 104)

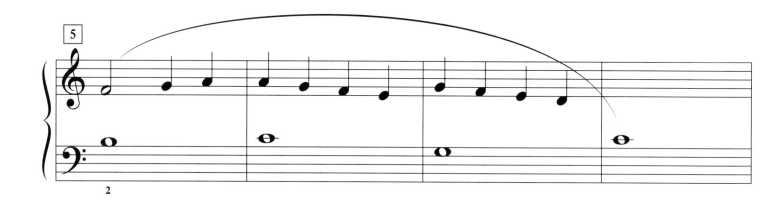

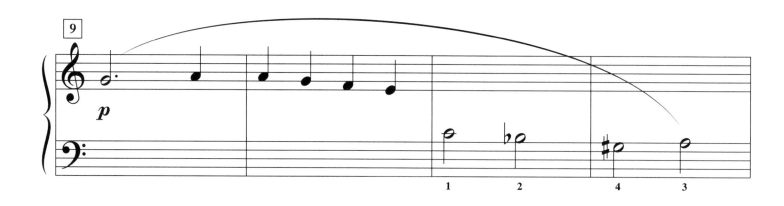

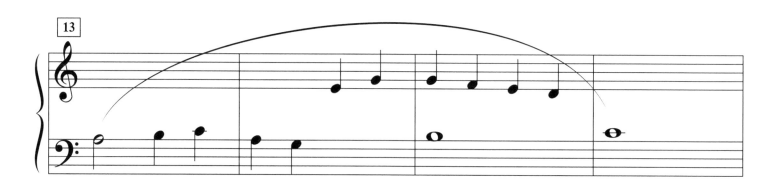

FF1697

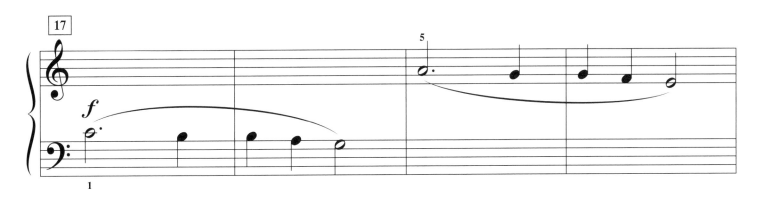

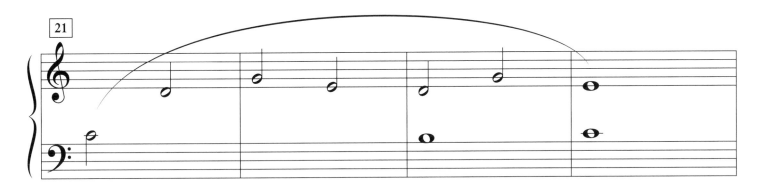

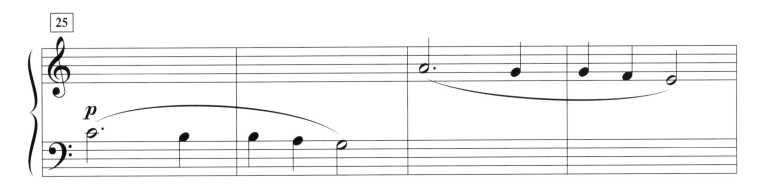

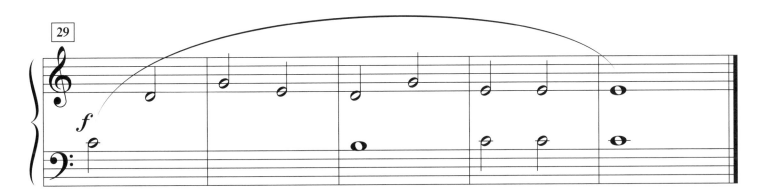

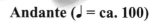

"SURPRISE" SYMPHONY

(Symphony in G major, Hob. 94, Movement Two)

Franz Joseph Haydn
arr. Mary Leaf

Andante (♩ = ca. 100)

Play all quarter notes slightly detached

Teacher Accompaniment: *(Student plays one octave higher)*

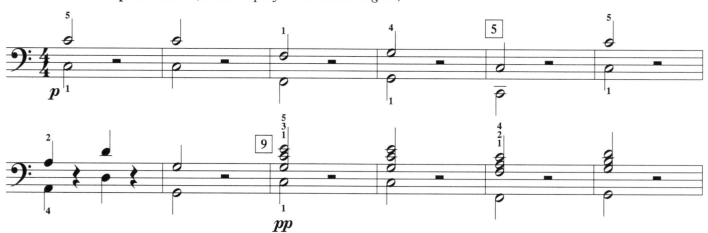

FF1697

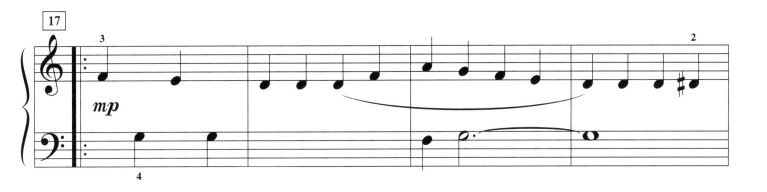

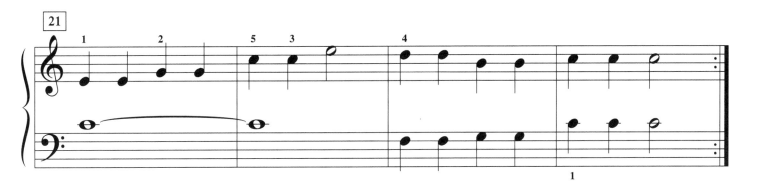

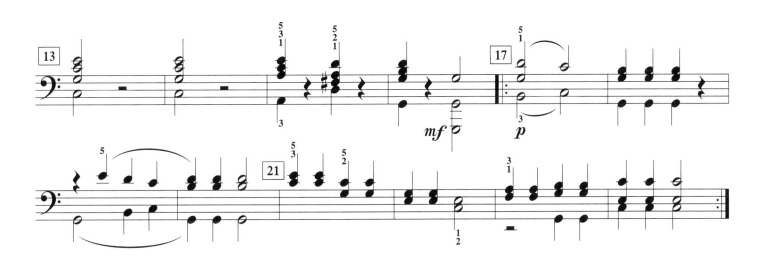

FINLANDIA
(Opus 26)

Jean Sibelius
arr. Kevin Costley

Andante (♩ = ca. 108)

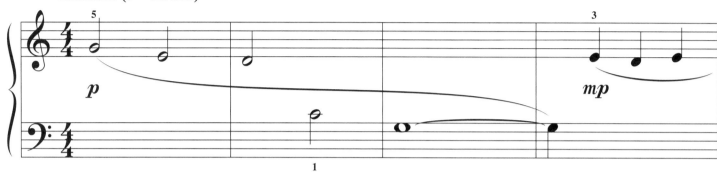

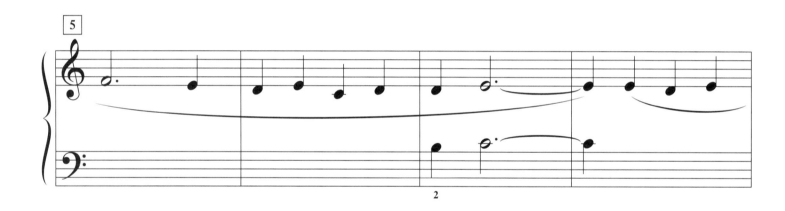

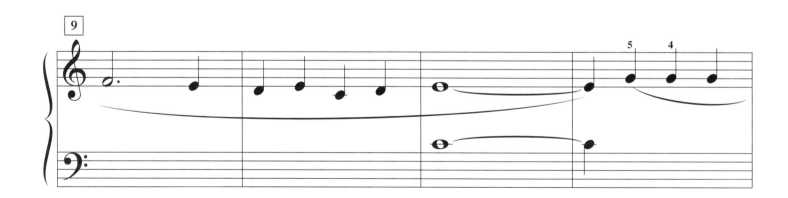

FF1697

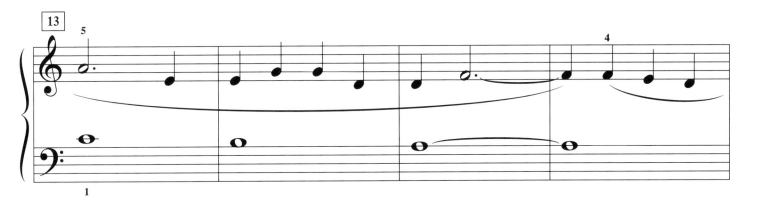

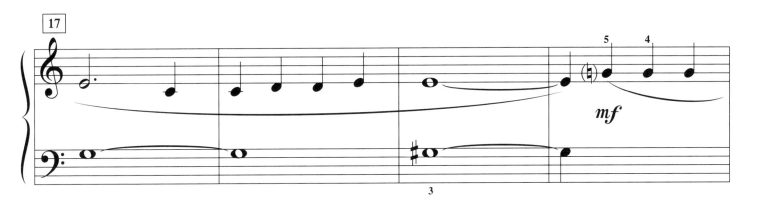

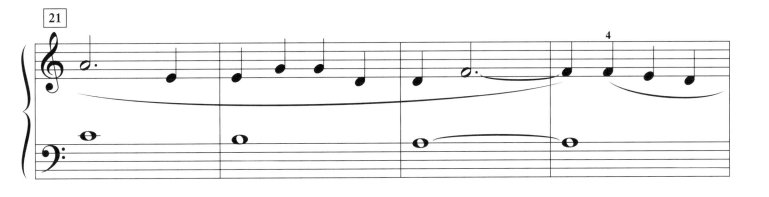

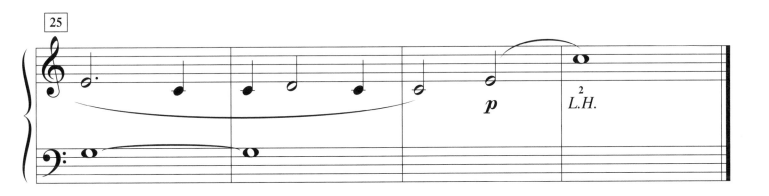

ROSES FROM THE SOUTH

Waltz 2 from *Das Spitzentuch der Königin, Opus 388*

Johann Strauss II
arr. Edwin McLean

Waltz tempo (♩. = ca. 60)

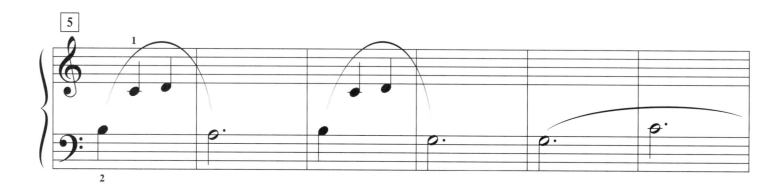

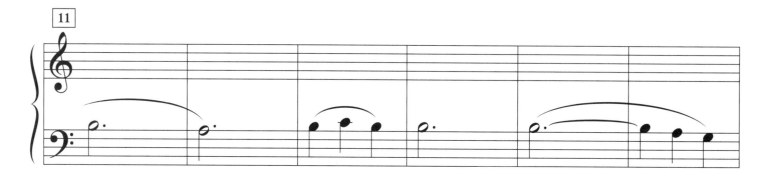

Teacher Accompaniment: (*Student plays one octave higher*)

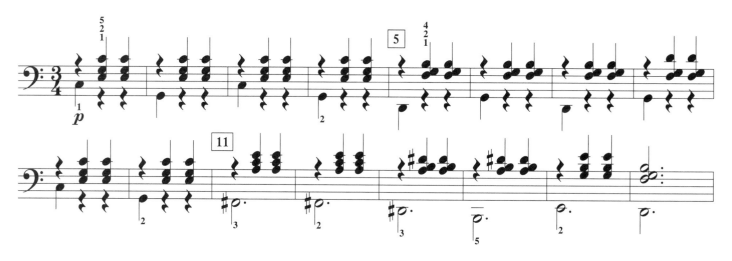

FF1697

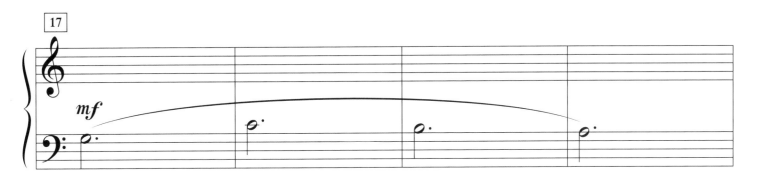

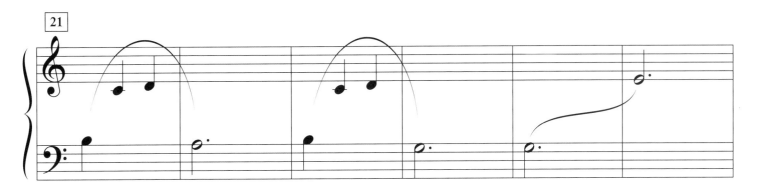

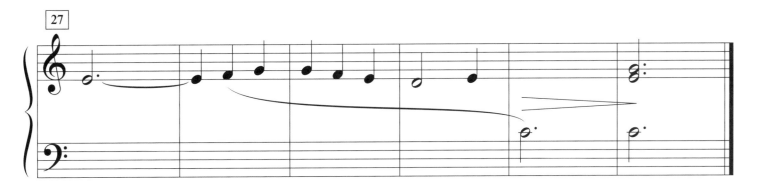

Theme from L'Arlésienne Suite
Secondo

Georges Bizet
arr. Emilie Lin

March tempo (♩ = ca. 112)

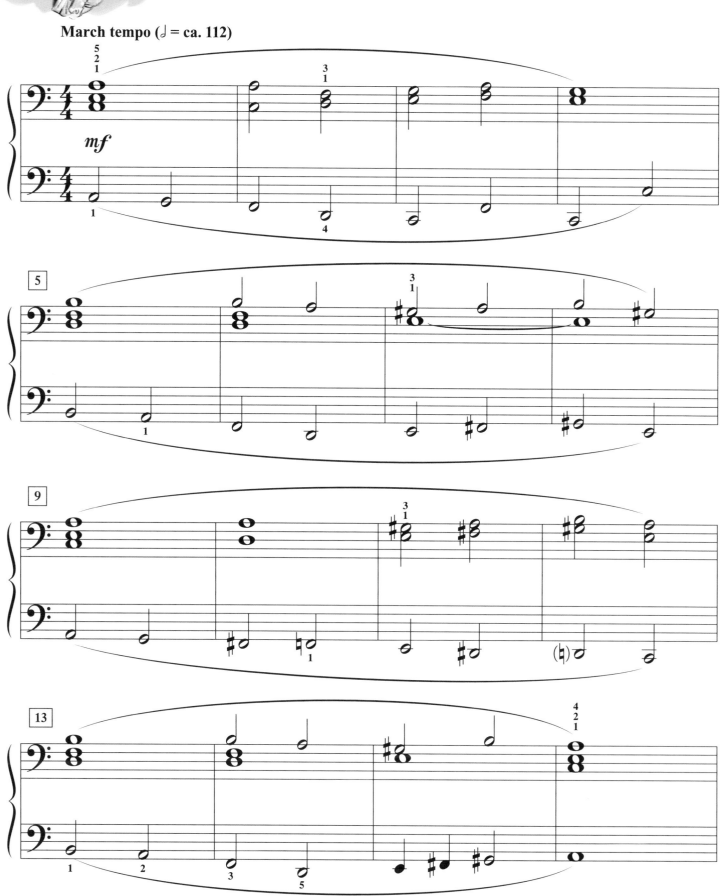

FF1697

Theme from L'Arlésienne Suite
Primo

Georges Bizet
arr. Emilie Lin

March tempo (♩ = ca. 112)

Play both hands 1 octave higher throughout

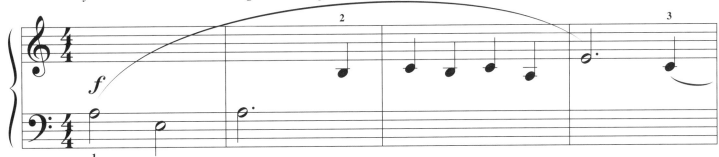

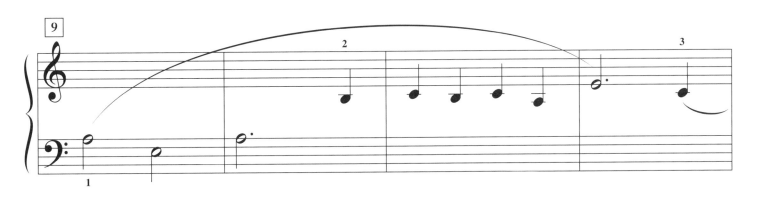

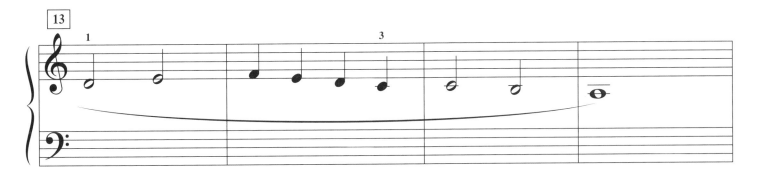

FF1697

31

Secondo

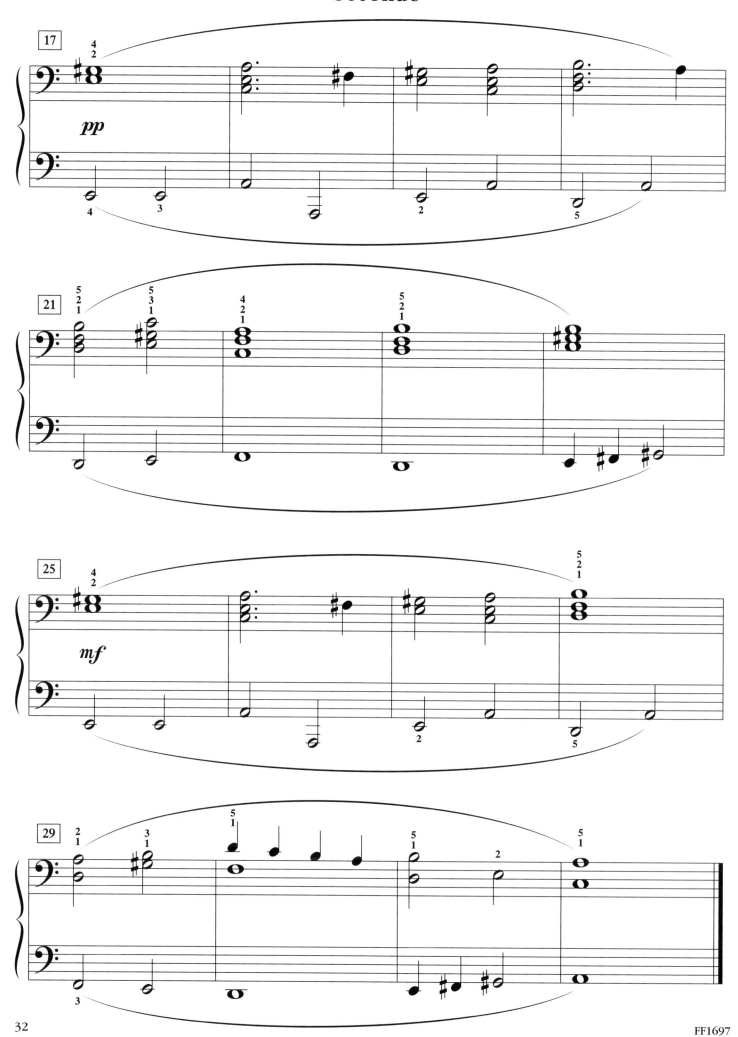

Primo

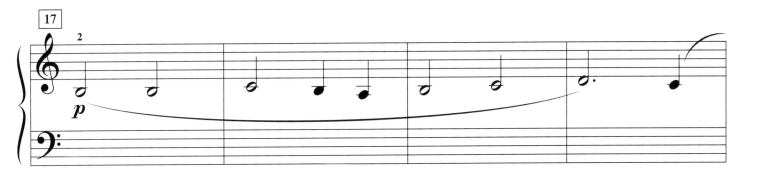

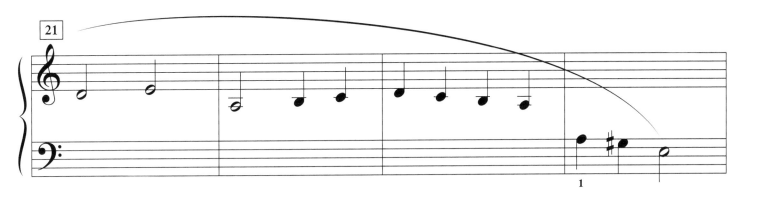

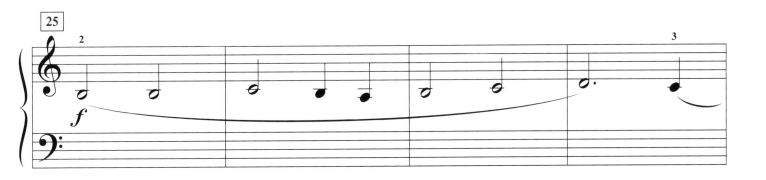

Alleluia, by Wolfgang Amadeus Mozart (1756-1791)

If you were to hear the original version of this piece, it would be sung by a soprano (a woman with a high voice). This *Alleluia* is from a larger piece called *Exsultate, jubilate,* and was written for soprano, orchestra, and organ. Can you imagine listening to all of these musicians making glorious sound together? Wolfgang Amadeus Mozart and his sister Anna Maria were both child prodigies, which means that they had great musical ability at a very early age. They performed throughout Europe, much to the joy of their audiences, as both of them played the harpsichord beautifully. During the years 1763-1773 the family toured Germany, France, England, and the Netherlands, performing before royalty, in private theatres, and in public concerts. They also spent considerable time in Vienna, Austria, which was considered the musical center of Europe.

"Surprise" Symphony, by Franz Joseph Haydn (1732-1809)

Franz Joseph Haydn was known as "Papa Haydn" because all of the musicians he worked with liked him so much. He worked for a royal family named Esterházy, and was in charge of composing and conducting his music for them. Some of his works are playful, as we hear in this theme. There is one place where the sound is *forte* instead of *mezzo piano*—can you hear it on the CD recording or when playing the piece? This is the "surprise!" In its original version, a small orchestra made up of strings, winds, brass, and timpani played this work.

Finlandia, by Jean Sibelius (1865-1957)

The ever-popular *Finlandia* was composed in 1899 as part of a suite for an orchestra entitled *Finland Awakens*. Finland won her independence from Russia in 1917, and Jean Sibelius was a composer who strove to create music that displayed the true spirit and patriotism of the Finnish people. Sibelius studied violin, and he and his brother and sister frequently made music together. He was educated in the first Finnish-speaking grammar school in Finland, and there became acquainted with Finnish mythology through the *Kalevala*, an epic book based on the ancient Finnish oral tradition of poetry and music.

Roses from the South, by Johann Strauss II (1825-1899)

Johann Strauss II was the son of an Austrian violinist, conductor, and composer. He was born and died in Vienna. Like his father, he became a violinist, conductor, and composer. He wrote a large number of waltzes, which were an important part of every day Austrian life. Besides *Roses from the South*, other famous waltzes he wrote include *The Blue Danube*, *A Thousand and One Nights*, and *Tales from the Vienna Woods*. This piece is from an operetta that takes place in Spain. It was premiered on October 1, 1880, in Vienna.

Theme from L'Arlésienne, by Georges Bizet (1838-1875)

L'Arlésienne is the French title that means *The Maid of Arles*. Arles is a town in Provence, which is a beautiful place in the south of France. The *L'Arlésienne Suite* was first performed October 1, 1872, in Paris, France. Would you like to have been there? Georges Bizet was born to musical parents, and showed extraordinary musical gifts when he was very young. He enrolled at the Paris Conservatory when he was only nine years old. He was a brilliant pianist, and composed fine piano music, church music, and songs. Bizet's opera *Carmen*, composed in 1873-1874, is one of the most popular operas ever written.

Timothy Brown

Composition has always been a natural form of self-expression for Timothy Brown. His Montessori-influenced philosophy has greatly helped define his approach as a teacher and composer of educational music. His composition originates from a love of improvisation at the piano and his personal goal of writing music that will help release the student's imagination.

Mr. Brown holds two degrees in piano performance, including a master's degree from the University of North Texas. His many honors include a "Commissioned for Clavier" magazine article, and first prize award in the Fifth Aliénor International Harpsichord Competition for his solo composition *Suite Española*. As a clinician, Mr. Brown has presented numerous clinics and most recently represented FJH Music with his presentation at the 2000 World Piano Pedagogy Conference. Currently living in Dallas, Mr. Brown teaches piano and composition at the Harry Stone Montessori Magnet School. He frequently serves as an adjudicator for piano and composition contests, and performs with his wife as duo-pianists.

Kevin Costley

Kevin Costley holds several graduate degrees in the areas of elementary education and piano pedagogy, and literature, including a doctorate from Kansas State University. For nearly two decades, he was owner and director of The Keyboard Academy, specializing in innovative small group instruction. Kevin served for several years as head of the music department and on the keyboard faculty of Messenger College in Joplin, Missouri.

Kevin is a standing faculty member of Inspiration Point Fine Arts Colony piano and string camp, where he performs and teaches private piano, ensemble classes, and composition. He conducts child development seminars, writes for national publications, serves as a clinician for piano workshops, and adjudicates numerous piano festivals and competitions. Presently, Dr. Costley is an assistant professor of early childhood education at Arkansas Tech University in Russellville, Arkansas.

Mary Leaf

Mary Leaf is an independent piano teacher specializing in early elementary through intermediate level students. She enjoys writing music that is descriptive, expressive, imaginative, and fun, while still being musically sound.

Mary received a music education degree from the University of Washington and has done continuing education in pedagogy at North Dakota State University. She has composed and arranged music for a family recorder ensemble, and has been active as a performer, accompanist, handbell ringer, and choir member at her church. She is also active in area contests as an accompanist. Mary and her husband Ron have five children and live in Bismarck, North Dakota.

FF1697

Emilie Lin

Emilie Lin shares her love of music through piano teaching, performing, composing, and arranging. Her goal as a composer and arranger is to create exciting, engaging pieces that make the process of learning and teaching music a fun and joyful adventure. As an independent music educator and cognitive psychologist, Emilie fosters her students' love of music by customizing curriculum according to each student's learning style, interests, and developmental stage. Guiding her students to become more conscientious during the learning process is also central to her teaching.

A *magna cum laude* from Carleton College, Emilie graduated with distinction in psychology and honors in music performance. In addition to her master's degree and Ph.D. degree in cognitive psychology from the University of Illinois (Urbana-Champaign), Emilie has a master's degree in piano performance with full scholarship from the University of Michigan. She has won concerto competitions at both Carleton College and the University of Michigan.

Emilie is a member of the Music Teachers National Association and has served as an adjudicator in local student events. She currently resides in Michigan with her husband Greg McConville and two sons, Peter and Ethan.

Edwin McLean

Edwin McLean is a freelance composer living in Chapel Hill, North Carolina. He is a graduate of the Yale School of Music, where he studied with Krzysztof Penderecki and Jacob Druckman. He also holds a master's degrees in music theory and a bachelor's degree in piano performance from the University of Colorado.

The recipient of several grants and awards: The MacDowell Colony, the John Work Award, the Woods Chandler Prize (Yale), Meet the Composer, Florida Arts Council, and others, he has also won the Aliénor Composition Competition for his work *Sonata for Harpsichord*, published by The FJH Music Company and recorded by Elaine Funaro (*Into the Millennium*, Gasparo GSCD-331).

Since 1979, Edwin McLean has arranged the music of some of today's best known recording artists. Currently, he is senior editor as well as MIDI orchestrator for FJH Music.

Kevin Olson

Kevin Olson is an active pianist, composer, and faculty member at Elmhurst College near Chicago, Illinois, where he teaches classical and jazz piano, music theory, and electronic music. He holds a Doctor of Education degree from National-Louis University, and bachelor's and master's degrees in music composition and theory from Brigham Young University. Before teaching at Elmhurst College, he held a visiting professor position at Humboldt State University in California.

A native of Utah, Kevin began composing at the age of five. When he was twelve, his composition *An American Trainride* received the Overall First Prize at the 1983 National PTA Convention in Albuquerque, New Mexico. Since then, he has been a composer-in-residence at the National Conference on Piano Pedagogy and has written music for the American Piano Quartet, Chicago a cappella, the Rich Matteson Jazz Festival, among others.

Kevin maintains a large piano studio, teaching students of a variety of ages and abilities. Many of the needs of his own piano students have inspired a diverse collection of books and solos published by The FJH Music Company Inc., which he joined as a writer in 1994.

Robert Schultz

Robert Schultz, composer, arranger, and editor, has achieved international fame during his career in the music publishing industry. The Schultz Piano Library, established in 1980, has included more than 500 publications of classical works, popular arrangements, and Schultz's original compositions in editions for pianists of every level from the beginner through the concert artist. In addition to his extensive library of published piano works, Schultz's output includes original orchestral works, chamber music, works for solo instruments, and vocal music.

Schultz has presented his published editions at workshops, clinics, and convention showcases throughout the United States and Canada. He is a long-standing member of ASCAP and has served as president of the Miami Music Teachers Association. Mr. Schultz's original piano compositions and transcriptions are featured on the compact disc recordings *Visions of Dunbar* and *Tina Faigen Plays Piano Transcriptions*, released on the ACA Digital label and available worldwide. His published original works for concert artists are noted in Maurice Hinson's *Guide to the Pianist's Repertoire, Third Edition*. He currently devotes his full time to composing and arranging, writing from his studio in Miami, Florida.

With your teacher, choose two or three of the classical themes from this book to play for an audience (it could be just for your teacher at the end of a lesson)!

Title of piece: Composer's Name:

_____

_____

_____

Listen to the CD recording of these pieces. Looking at your list of pieces above, which one is your favorite? Mark it with a star.

In the space below, draw a picture of what this music sounds like to you!

Now you can prepare for another classical theme playing event!